THE
BELIEF
CHALLENGE

ROXANNE TUOMELA

AWARD-WINNING AUTHOR
MEMBER OF THE 2% CLUB

BEEZER BOOKS
Beezer Books

To My Husband and Our Children,

Think positively,
welcome change,
pray, have complete faith,
be believers,
and together
we will manifest everything we desire.

All My Love,

Roxanne/Mom

Foreword

I am the creator of my own life. I have manifested everything, everyone, and every experience in my life, good or bad. I trained myself to think about what I wished to have rather than think about what I did not want. I learned how to constantly update my beliefs, which had been instilled in me, so I could stop unwanted patterns in order to experience something new and positive. I tapped deeply into my spirituality by connecting with God and my angels through letters I wrote to them asking for exactly what I wanted in my life. I created manifestation stations and had complete faith that I would receive everything I desired. I am a master at manifesting. I am living the life of my dreams.

Introduction

Dear God and my Angels,

I am grateful I have been assigned to help others connect with you. With your guidance, I will help others learn how to update their belief system in order to experience the changes they desire. I will teach others how to manifest abundant love, happiness and wealth, safety and security, and how to manifest a loving family/tribe/community through written requests and prayers addressed to you.

Thank you for this opportunity to help others.

All my love, faith, and gratitude,

Roxanne

Table of Contents

CHAPTER 1

Understanding Your Beliefs and Recognizing What Needs to Change

What are you desiring to achieve? What do you long for in your life? Are you praying for big things or for something simple? Do you feel safe and secure? Do you see yourself in a particular career? Do you wish for fame and fortune? Are you hoping for change? Do you hope to become more spiritual? Do you want to make a better connection with God/your Higher Power? Are you aware that angels have been assigned to you and are waiting patiently for your request(s)? Do you wish for love in your life? If you could be anywhere in the world, where would you like to be? Where do you belong? What are some of the beliefs which were instilled in you as a child?

Are you ready to update your belief(s) in order to experience a different outcome?

Definition of the word "belief" according to the Merriam-Webster dictionary: 1) a state or habit of mind in which trust or confidence is placed in some person or thing; 2) something that is accepted, considered to be true, or held as an opinion; 3) a conviction of the truth of some statement or the reality of some being or phenomenon, especially when based on examination of evidence.

The first task at hand is to get clear on what your beliefs are. The only way for you to experience changes in your life is to be willing to take the necessary steps to update some of your beliefs which were, quite possibly, instilled in you dating back to the time you were a child. Let go of any fears that you may hurt someone else's feelings if you find their belief is not serving you well. It's okay to update or tweak your belief system; if you don't, you will possibly end up hurting yourself.

To uncover some of your current beliefs, please write down answers to the following:

What belief(s) immediately come to mind which were taught to you as a child?

_____

_____

_____

_____

_____

_____

_____

_____

_____

_____

What are you currently experiencing which you no longer wish to experience?

_____

_____

_____

_____

_____

_____

_____

_____

_____

_____

What do you wish to manifest?

_____

_____

_____

_____

_____

_____

_____

_____

_____

_____

_____

How is your connection with God and your angels?

_____

_____

_____

_____

_____

_____

_____

_____

_____

_____

_____

LOVE MANIFESTATION STATION

CHAPTER 2

Get Clear on Your Beliefs Surrounding Love

Are you wishing to manifest more joy and happiness into your life? Many things can bring us joy and happiness, but the most powerful form of happiness can be found through LOVE. Love can be experienced between a man and a woman, a man and a man, a woman and a woman, a parent/grandparent and a child, between brother(s) and sister(s), friends, neighbors, between a pet and their owner—the list goes on and on.

When we give and receive love, *everything* else falls into place. There is incredible energy that comes with love; you can actually *feel* it. That positive energy is very helpful when manifesting.

I challenge you to open your heart to loving and being loved.

What is your belief when it comes to true love and how to give and receive it?

_____

_____

_____

_____

_____

_____

_____

_____

_____

_____

Each and every man I have loved has been unique in his own way. I have gained so much in my life by opening up my heart to experience all kinds of love. It took me nearly three decades to figure out what I truly desired in a relationship.

I had to uncover the patterns I was repeating and decipher what my belief was. I needed to look back to understand *who* I was manifesting and *why*.

Growing up, my parents' belief was that I would

experience great joy and stability if I were to fall in love with a highly educated white-collar professional type of man. More than once I was in such a relationship, and in the beginning, monetary wealth did provide security, but it did not bring me the joy I was longing for.

I realized I was manifesting the wrong man for me. I needed to update the belief my parents had instilled in me. I asked myself what kind of love I should choose to manifest and I asked God for his help. On a daily basis, I lit my candle in my manifestation station, took out pen and paper, and wrote to God and to my angels. I asked for my ideal match. I pulled guardian angel cards for further clarity on what I should expect to experience.

I manifested my perfect match. When he first came into my life I was thinking he was everything I wasn't looking for, because I defaulted to my old belief. It turns out he was everything I was needing in my life. God placed him in my life, and my prayers were answered. I am now experiencing a love that brings me tremendous joy and security; we do belong together.

My belief surrounding love is no longer about

level of education or job title. My true love recipe is made up of special "ingredients" which my man, today, is made up of. He is trustworthy, stable, hardworking, smart, a provider, smart with his money, lives within his means, kind, supportive, a "tender paw" yet a man's man, talented, faithful, exciting, interesting, a teacher/guide/mentor; he is independent, a simple man, and full of passion. All of these characteristics are what I believe to be my perfect love. I thank God for my love life, and I am grateful for the angels who assisted me on my journey to love.

End result: Changing my belief has positively changed my experience.

Who loves you?

_____

_____

_____

_____

_____

_____

_____

_____

_____

_____

Who do you love?

_____

_____

_____

_____

_____

_____

_____

_____

_____

_____

What belief did your parent(s)/guardian(s) instill in you about what true love is supposed to be or what it is supposed to look like?

_____

_____

_____

_____

_____

_____

_____

_____

_____

Have you witnessed others in love? Were your parents in love? Or did find your friends' parents demonstrate a love life you would rather experience? Whose love life do you admire?

_____

_____

_____

_____

_____

_____

_____

_____

_____

_____

Is your current belief serving you well in love? Is your love life ideal, or are you desiring a different kind of love experience?

_____

_____

_____

_____

_____

_____

_____

_____

_____

_____

What are you experiencing?

_____
_____
_____
_____
_____
_____
_____
_____
_____
_____
_____

What do you believe you need and want in a partner?

_____
_____
_____
_____
_____
_____
_____
_____
_____
_____
_____
_____

What are the "special ingredients" you desire in a mate?

_____

_____

_____

_____

_____

_____

_____

_____

_____

_____

_____

Are you feeling safe and secure?

_____

_____

_____

_____

_____

_____

_____

_____

_____

_____

_____

Do you have a sense of belonging?

_____

_____

_____

_____

_____

_____

_____

_____

_____

_____

_____

Are your repeating any unwanted pattern?

_____

_____

_____

_____

_____

_____

_____

_____

_____

_____

_____

Do you recall your first love?

_____

_____

_____

_____

_____

_____

_____

_____

_____

_____

What did the experience mean to you?

_____

_____

_____

_____

_____

_____

_____

_____

_____

_____

_____

Have your thoughts about the experience changed over time?

_____

_____

_____

_____

_____

_____

_____

_____

_____

_____

_____

What did you learn from it?

_____

_____

_____

_____

_____

_____

_____

_____

_____

_____

What direction did your life take?

_____

_____

_____

_____

_____

_____

_____

_____

_____

_____

_____

If you could do things differently, what would you have done differently?

_____

_____

_____

_____

_____

_____

_____

_____

_____

_____

Do you have any regrets?

_____

_____

_____

_____

_____

_____

_____

_____

_____

_____

Now that you have had an opportunity to get more clarity about what kind of love you wish to manifest, do you need to update your belief(s)? I challenge you to create a new belief about love for *you*.

Create a love manifestation station and to write to God and your angels for what you want to manifest and request they give you guidance. Then watch for signs—signs that are pointing you in the direction you should to go. Manifest the love. Have faith and believe love is out there waiting for you to give it and receive it. Then, give thanks for the love you manifest.

HARVEST MANIFESTATION STATION

CHAPTER 3

Get Clear on Your Beliefs Surrounding Good Health and Body Image

Are you healthy? Do you love your body? Do you enjoy working out/exercising? Could you be nourishing your body differently for optimal health and/or performance? Are there any family health history issues which you are concerned about? Growing up, what were your family's beliefs surrounding good health and your body? What belief was instilled in you regarding the following:

What should your body look like?

_____

_____

_____

_____

_____

_____

_____

_____

_____

_____

_____

What do you consider to be healthy living?

_____

_____

_____

_____

_____

_____

_____

_____

_____

_____

_____

What is your picture of good health?

_____

_____

_____

_____

_____

_____

_____

_____

_____

_____

When I was a young woman, beliefs surrounding my body were instilled by my dad. His intentions were good—he really wanted the best for me—but I ended up pretty unhealthy as a result.

Growing up, I believed I needed to look like the Barbie doll I was playing with; I grew up in the "Mad Men" era. In the 1960s, my dad was a commercial art director for one of the largest advertising agencies in the world. He was surrounded by curvaceous models and messages of what a woman should look like to experience joy, happiness, and success. When my dad introduced me to others, he would say, "This is my daughter,

Roxanne, The Body." I believed I needed to have the perfect body.

For decades I suffered internally. I had constant, fearful thoughts over foods I ate with my friends. As teenagers, my best friend and I would scarf down a box of macaroni and cheese or a pan of brownies, and then I'd pop diet pills to attempt to be at the "perfect" weight.

I was sabotaging the joy and happiness of late-night munching with my friends. I was manifesting a constant roller coaster of weight gain and weight loss with yo-yo dieting and my thoughts. I needed to rethink the belief which had been instilled in me, but I wasn't clear on what exactly brought me the most joy, happiness, and success.

In my thirties, after the loss of my parents and birth of my children, I realized my figure was not my road to joy, happiness and success—it was being a healthy, happy, successful mom. Longevity became my primary focus. Thus, I manifested a healthy and fun-filled lifestyle. My new belief was to live a life of *health admired, weight desired*.

Do you desire to be healthy? Do you appreciate and love your body?

_____

_____

_____

_____

_____

_____

_____

_____

_____

_____

Who in your life would benefit if you were in good health? How would they benefit?

_____

_____

_____

_____

_____

_____

_____

_____

_____

_____

My new belief had me exploring what living my healthiest lifestyle would entail for me. I no longer obsessed over my figure in the mirror, but instead, focused on being admired more for my healthful appearance. I thought about all the wonderful benefits I would experience, such as:

- phenomenal blood work results, such as healthy cholesterol, blood pressure, etc.
- zero medications
- being disease free
- off-the-chain intimacy
- confidence
- pleasure in physically challenging activities like hunting, biking, marathons

I created my healthy-living manifestation station and wrote to God and my angels. I asked for help in discovering what would be best for me, as a bio-individual, to live a healthier lifestyle in order to live a long, abundant life in a body that I would be proud of. My prayers were answered. I got educated on living a life in balance, and I manifested all of the benefits that came along with my new belief system: health admired, weight desired.

Is it time for you to update your belief surrounding your body and your lifestyle? What does being healthy mean to you?

*List some of the benefits you would experience if
you chose to be your healtiest version of yourself.*

_____

_____

_____

_____

_____

_____

_____

_____

_____

_____

*What other areas of your life would benefit or
improve if you were the healthiest you could be,
if you were at your ideal weight, if you felt your
absolute best?*

_____

_____

_____

_____

_____

_____

_____

_____

_____

_____

Now is the time for you to manifest perfect health for yourself. Bring thoughts and energy to being healthy, not ill. Create a healthy-living manifestation station for yourself. Write to God and your angels and ask them to help you improve upon your eating habits and your exercise routine. Have total faith that you will manifest a healthier you. Think only about having a strong and beautiful body. Push out any negative thoughts about your body. Stop thinking about what you don't want. Think only about what you do want.

CAREER MANIFESTATION STATION

CHAPTER 4

Get Clear on Your Beliefs Surrounding Education/ Work/Career/Purpose

Where are you at this stage of your life? Are you content, or are you wishing for change? If you are in high school, are you clear on which college you want to attend? If you were accepted into the school at the top of your wish list, would it be a dream come true? If you are currently enrolled in a college/university, do you believe you are taking the right courses for your end goal? Do you find you are already wanting to change your major? Maybe you're not a student but wish to be one—do you want to manifest that?

Perhaps you're already a graduate. Do you love

your job? Do you feel you are in the right career? Are you fulfilling your purpose? Do you
even know what your purpose is? Are you happy?
If you aren't happy, are you ready to move on,
or are you terrified to make a change? Are you
money-driven? Service-driven? Does your title
mean something to you, or is it more important
to someone else? What drives you?

*Whose belief has played a part in where you are
today?*

_____
_____
_____
_____
_____
_____
_____
_____
_____
_____
_____
_____

There was no tremendous pressure placed on
me, as a kid, as to what I was supposed to be
when I grew up. I truly do not recall any belief

instilled in me in this area of my life. For thirty years I have searched for that one job, that one career, that one opportunity to truly love what I do. And, here I am! I am a master at manifesting, and my amazing calling is to help others manifest their happiest, healthiest life. As always, take time to reflect upon what you have been taught. The beliefs instilled in you—have they placed you where you really want to be? Or is it time to change your belief surrounding education/work/career/purpose?

What has been instilled in you, according to your family's belief, regarding education?

_____

_____

_____

_____

_____

_____

_____

_____

_____

_____

_____

_____

Are you enjoying your courses?

_____

_____

_____

_____

_____

_____

_____

_____

_____

_____

_____

Do you attend a brick and mortar school, or do you take classes online?

_____

_____

_____

_____

_____

_____

_____

_____

_____

_____

_____

_____

Are you happy?

_____

_____

_____

_____

_____

_____

_____

_____

_____

_____

What beliefs were instilled in you as a child about the kind of work you should be doing or what career you should pursue?

_____

_____

_____

_____

_____

_____

_____

_____

_____

_____

Are you satisfied with the work that you do? Do you enjoy your career?

_____

_____

_____

_____

_____

_____

_____

_____

_____

_____

I am what is referred to as a "Jack of all trades." I was extremely successful at landing any job I went after because, at an early age, I had the ability to envision myself in the role before receiving the offer. It's been an interesting journey, and every experience has brought value to my life. I have learned a tremendous amount by not being afraid to make changes along the way. I know I would not be where I am today had I stayed with one job.

Get clear on what you should be doing with your life with regards to your schooling, work/career, your purpose.

What jobs have you had and what did you learn from each experience?"

_____

_____

_____

_____

_____

_____

_____

_____

_____

_____

Here is what I discovered about myself in all the jobs I have had and what I experienced:

Envelope stuffer: My first job, first paycheck; save money to spend money; proud of myself.

Babysitter: I discovered I am responsible, nurturing, creative, and fun.

Admin Assistant/Executive Assistant: I provided support and helped others shine.

Membership Director: I found true appreciation for my beautiful surroundings; I learned that it's healthy to invest in passions that bring you happiness.

Customer Service Rep: I learned to be grateful for opportunities and accept them; I gained skill to learn and apply knowledge on how to adapt to each and every individual and situation.

Marketing Manager: Plastic surgeons and cosmetic surgeons have different priorities, talents and gifts; entrepreneurs are eccentric, successful, and caring individuals.

Medical Transcriptionist: I wanted a job that allowed me to be at home with my firstborn. THIS was probably the first time I understood how to manifest what I truly desired. I thought about what I wanted, I prayed for it, and did what it was going to take to get it done. I got certified in medical transcribing, I worked out of my home, I was with my kids, and I helped to provide for my family.

Daycare Assistant: Stable income with benefits, still with my son at my side.

Professional Packer: I am not afraid to move, and I do it well.

Health/Life Coach: Here, again, I manifested the work I love to do and from my own home office; I will FOREVER enjoy helping others live their happiest, healthiest life.

Outside Sales: The more I put into it, the more I got out of it. There is no limit to the amount one can earn. Helping others with their biggest investment is rewarding work.

Retail Sales: Competition is a double-edged sword. NEVER stay in a toxic environment. Selling adventure is a blast.

Recruiter: It feels good to help others become gainfully employed.

Author: Sharing what I know and what I have learned to help others. Loving that I can write wherever my family and I are, and whenever I choose to, even if that's at 3 a.m.

Entrepreneur: I am a "2%'er". I do what I love. Being brave enough to go after what one desires to manifest and having total faith that it will come, it will be achieved.

Master Manifestor: I am the creator of my life. My beliefs have created my experiences, and all of my experiences have confirmed my beliefs. I learned from my own mentors that in order for my experiences to change, I needed to update my beliefs. Anything I want to experience and obtain I can and will through love, faith, and gratitude for God and my angels.

Mother and Wife: The best and most rewarding experience of them all! The titles I am most proud of.

What is your belief about your current or past job/career?

_____

_____

_____

_____

_____

_____

_____

_____

_____

_____

Is your title important to you, and why?

_____

_____

_____

_____

_____

_____

_____

_____

_____

_____

*What is your belief about income/health benefits/
retirement?*

_____

_____

_____

_____

_____

_____

_____

_____

_____

_____

_____

What is your definition of wealth?

_____

_____

_____

_____

_____

_____

_____

_____

_____

_____

_____

Do you love your job?

_____

_____

_____

_____

_____

_____

_____

_____

_____

_____

Are you okay with finding another job, or are you frightened to make a change? Why?

_____

_____

_____

_____

_____

_____

_____

_____

_____

_____

_____

Is your fear there because of your belief system?

_____

_____

_____

_____

_____

_____

_____

_____

_____

_____

*What would happen if what paralyzed you
didn't actually exist? Where are your thoughts?
Remember, whatever you think about, you are
bringing energy to it.*

_____

_____

_____

_____

_____

_____

_____

_____

_____

What do you believe is your purpose?

_____

_____

_____

_____

_____

_____

_____

_____

_____

_____

Can you see now, after much practice, that it's okay and necessary to update some of your beliefs? You are not hurting anyone. In fact, your loved ones, God, and your angels want nothing more than for you to live your happiest, healthiest life.

It is time to create your manifestation station to manifest your destiny regarding school/work/career, your purpose. Light your candle and write to God and your angels. Be very specific with what you want to be doing with your skills, your talents; ask for the experience you wish to have. Keep all thoughts on what you want; do not think about what you do not want. Have complete faith that you will receive exactly what you are praying for.

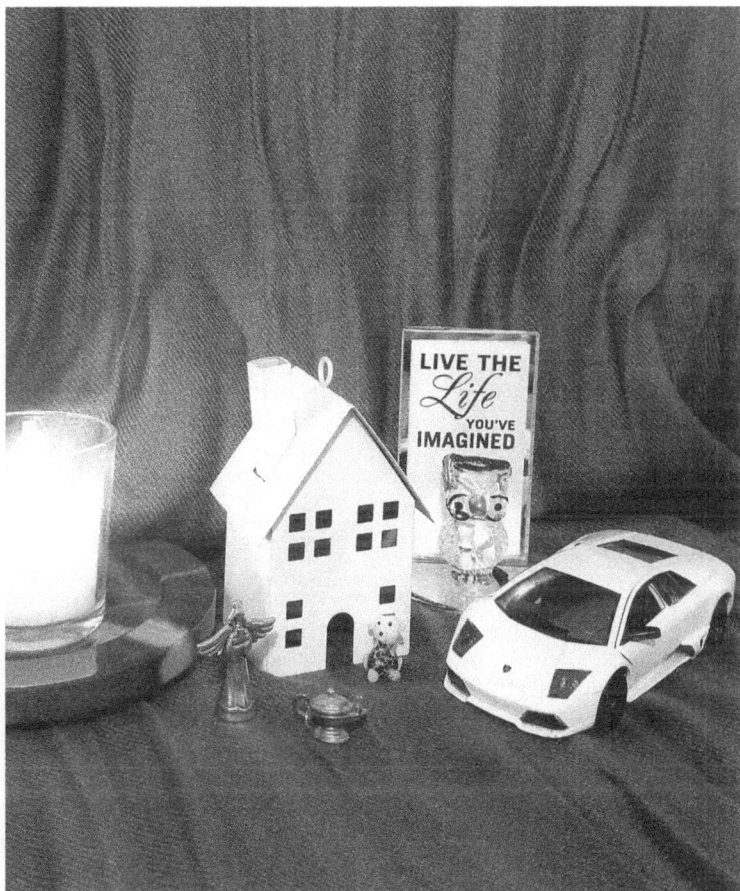

DREAM BIG MANIFESTATION STATION

CHAPTER 5

Get Clear on Your Beliefs Surrounding Home Life/ Belonging

What are your beliefs surrounding your home life? Were you brought up to believe it's best to stay in one place for your entire upbringing, or were you told change is good, that you will learn how to adapt to change? There is no right or wrong answer. You and friends may have completely different experiences. Besides your home life, which group of friends are you associated with? Do their values meet yours? Is your life richer because of the people in your life or quite the opposite? The question to ask yourself is whether the beliefs instilled in you as a kid serve you well today.

My own childhood experience was one on the move, and my changing of location went on for years after I left home. I have lived in ten states from north to south, east to west; I have had over thirty addresses. No, we weren't in the witness protection program, nor was my father in the military; my BFF lovingly calls me her "gypsy friend." One of my strengths today, because of the number of places I have lived, is that I adapt easily to change. I like that belief, and it still serves me well today. I also had a belief that I would become bored without change. Just like my mentors had taught me, my beliefs have created my experiences, and my experiences have confirmed my beliefs.

For the first time in my life, I have settled into a home, in a place, where I have never felt more comfort and stability, and I am far from bored. It feels amazing. My new belief involves me living in my truth. Truthfully, I am most content living away from it all. I no longer need to have a change of address to experience myself thriving. My man and I manifested the perfect home and location for our family. We envisioned exactly what we wished for. I created our home-sweet-home manifestation station, and together we manifested where we are today. We love our home. We love the "tribe" of friends we associate with, with whom we share a mindset and values. We are all thriving. We have love, we are safe and secure, and we have a sense of belonging that fills our hearts and souls.

What is family?

_____

_____

_____

_____

_____

_____

_____

_____

_____

Who is your family?

_____

_____

_____

_____

_____

_____

_____

_____

_____

What are you experiencing with your family?

_____

_____

_____

_____

_____

_____

_____

_____

_____

_____

_____

_____

Who are your friends?

_____

_____

_____

_____

_____

_____

_____

_____

_____

_____

_____

_____

What are you experiencing with your friends?

_____

_____

_____

_____

_____

_____

_____

_____

_____

_____

Have they been your friend for a lifetime, a season, a reason, or for a "chapter" in your life?

_____

_____

_____

_____

_____

_____

_____

_____

_____

_____

*What are you experiencing with your spouse/
boyfriend/girlfriend/significant other?*

_____

_____

_____

_____

_____

_____

_____

_____

_____

_____

*Do you feel safe and secure in your relationships?
Why or why not?*

_____

_____

_____

_____

_____

_____

_____

_____

_____

_____

_____

What does it mean to belong?

_____

_____

_____

_____

_____

_____

_____

_____

_____

_____

Where do you wish to belong?

_____

_____

_____

_____

_____

_____

_____

_____

_____

_____

Which "tribe" do you belong to or wish to belong to?

_____

_____

_____

_____

_____

_____

_____

_____

_____

_____

_____

Are you surrounding yourself with others who are in alignment with your values?

_____

_____

_____

_____

_____

_____

_____

_____

_____

_____

The individuals you surround yourself with, what purpose do they serve in your life?

_____

_____

_____

_____

_____

_____

_____

_____

_____

_____

CHAPTER 6

Summing Things Up

The process of manifesting is the same for all areas of your life. I want you to be very aware of your thoughts, and if your thoughts are filled with worry and negativity you must do a paradigm shift. Release all your fears and worries and negativity to God and your angels. Ask for their help. Do a "belief check" surrounding the area of your life where you want change or a different outcome; is it time to quit repeating unwanted patterns? Again, always reflect upon what belief was instilled in you to help you recognize where you may need to update such beliefs. Is the original belief serving you well, or do you need to update that belief? Create your manifestation station, and on a daily basis write out your wishes, your desires, your requests to God and your angels. *Believe* that with complete faith, you will experience exactly what you want in your life. *This* is a *belief* which I hope to instill in *you*!

What have you been focusing on lately?

_____

_____

_____

_____

_____

_____

_____

_____

_____

_____

What have you been experiencing in your life?

_____

_____

_____

_____

_____

_____

_____

_____

_____

_____

Are you bringing energy to the right things?

_____

_____

_____

_____

_____

_____

_____

_____

_____

_____

Have your thoughts been positive or negative?

_____

_____

_____

_____

_____

_____

_____

_____

_____

_____

Is your glass half full or half empty? Is it partly cloudy or partly sunny? In other words, are you an optimist or a pessimist?

_____

_____

_____

_____

_____

_____

_____

_____

_____

_____

What would you rather be experiencing?

_____

_____

_____

_____

_____

_____

_____

_____

_____

_____

_____

What else are you experiencing in your life?

_____

_____

_____

_____

_____

_____

_____

_____

_____

_____

Remember, what you think about or where you put your energy is exactly what the universe will deliver for you. Think about only the experiences you want; do not think about what you do not want. For instance, if you are worrying about your next doctor's visit and all that you can think about is bad news, well, what do you think you will receive? Rather than gloom and doom, why not have total faith knowing you will receive nothing but good news?

Changing one's mindset can take time and practice . . . or, perhaps, that's just one's belief. Actually, once you get in the practice of being aware of your thoughts and you get good at doing a paradigm shift, the direct outcome of what you are wishing for will come much more quickly and easily, and your experiences will be exactly what you desire.

Create your manifestation state, write to God and ask Him to assign you your angels, and ask for what you want to achieve with their help.

TRAVEL MANIFESTATION STATION

CHAPTER 7

Time to Manifest It!

1. Pick a quiet and sacred place to set up your manifestation station. Within your station add a candle, an angel figure or figurines and any other items that resemble what you are trying to manifest.

2. To begin to connect to your God/Higher Power or Spirit Guide and your angels, light your candle.

3. Once you've have lit your candle, pull out a blank journal and write to them. Write them a thank you letter as if you have already received what it is that you are trying to manifest in your life or in the lives of others.

From here on out, have *complete faith* and *believe* that you will manifest anyone, anything and every experience into your life.

Remember, you must first get clear on your beliefs and whether or not they still serve you or whether it's time to update them. Create your manifestaton station and ask for what it is that you desire.

Please be sure to **CELEBRATE** every time you manifest! And, I promise you, in no time, with practice, you, too, will become a master at manifesting.

With love, faith, and gratitude,

Master Manifestor

www.ingramcontent.com/pod-product-compliance
Lightning Source LLC
Chambersburg PA
CBHW022037090426
42741CB00007B/1106